THE DOMINIE WORLD OF ANIMALS

BABOONS

Graham Meadows & Claire Vial

Contents

DOMINIE PRESS
Pearson Learning Group

About Baboons

Baboons are really very big monkeys. They belong to a large and **diverse** group of animals called primates. Other members of this same group include orangutans, chimpanzees, gorillas, and humans.

Baboons are found in many parts of Africa. There are several different types of baboons. Each type has a different name.

This book is about the savanna baboon.

Swahili is a language that is spoken in many parts of East Africa. The Swahili word for *baboon* is *nyani*.

Where They Live

Baboons live in many different types of **habitats**, ranging from woodlands to grassy plains. They can **adapt** to almost any habitat—even very dry areas—as long as they have enough food to eat and enough water to drink.

Their habitat must include safe places where they can rest during the day and sleep at night. They usually feed during the day and sleep in trees or on cliffs at night.

Baboons sleep high in the trees or on cliffs so they can keep out of the reach of **predators**.

Their Shape and Size

A baboon's head is shaped like that of a dog, with a long **muzzle**, or mouth and nose. Baboons have very powerful jaws. Their eyes are set close together, below large ridges of bone called brow ridges.

Male baboons are larger and heavier than females and have a **ruff**, or ring of long hair, around the neck. An adult male baboon can be up to thirty inches in height at the shoulders and weigh as much as 100 pounds. Adult female baboons are shorter and usually weigh about half as much as males. The females have no ruff.

A baboon's tail can be almost three feet long.

Their Diet

Baboons are **omnivores**. This means they eat both plants and animals. They use their hands to eat and to dig up roots and bulbs. Grass is a large part of their **diet**. Baboons eat other plant foods, including leaves, flowers, fruits and berries, seeds, shoots, twigs, bark, and mushrooms.

A baboon's diet also includes grasshoppers, spiders, lizards, frogs, fish, birds' eggs, and small mammals.

When They Mate

Female baboons mature and start to **mate** when they are about five years old. Males take about twice as long to mature, usually when they are about ten years old.

Baboons can mate at any time of the year, but they usually mate during rainy seasons. That is when they are strongest and more food is available.

Female baboons give birth about six months after they mate.

Female baboons spend up to half of their adult lives caring for babies, and about one-third of their adult lives pregnant.

Their Young

Female baboons usually give birth at night. They normally have one baby at a time; twins are rare. A newborn baboon has a bright pink face, pink ears, and black hair. Its face and ears become darker when the baby reaches three to four months of age. By the time the baby is six months old, its face is the same color as an adult baboon's.

During the first month of the baby's life, the female uses one hand to hold the newborn next to her stomach while she is moving.

A baboon's eyes are open at birth.

Their Young

When a baby baboon is about five to six weeks old, it is carried on its mother's back. The baby hangs on with its hands and feet. Once it is about twelve weeks old, the baby can sit up on its mother's back and ride "jockey" style, like a person riding a horse.

When it reaches four to six months of age, a baboon begins to spend most of its time with other young baboons. By the time it is one year old, the baby is almost **independent** from its mother. But it will still depend on its mother for protection for another six months.

Baboons can live up to thirty years in the **wild**.

Their Families

Baboons live in large family groups called troops. The members of a troop sleep, travel, and eat together. There are usually thirty to forty baboons in a troop, but a single family group can include as many as fifty animals. Within one troop, there may be seven or eight males and about twice as many females, along with their young. Females spend their lives in the troop into which they were born. But males often leave the troop and join another group when they are about four years old.

Each baboon troop has a home range, or special area in which it lives.

A Day in the Life of a Baboon

In the Morning

An hour or so after sunrise, baboons make their way down from the safety of the trees or cliffs where they spent the night. While the young baboons play, the adults sit in pairs or small groups, warming themselves in the sun and **grooming** each other.

When they've finished grooming, they begin to move, walking on all four limbs. As they move along, they spread out and start to forage, or look for food. They stop to rest during the hottest part of the day.

During the day, a baboon troop may travel more than five miles.

A Day in the Life of a Baboon

In the Afternoon

Later in the afternoon, when the air is cooler, the baboons start to forage again. While they are spread out, they keep an eye out for predators such as leopards and cheetahs. If a baboon sees a predator, it calls out an alarm, warning the other baboons in the troop.

Baboons get a lot of water from the food they eat, and by licking the dew that forms on their fur during the night.

Baboons use more than thirty different sounds to **communicate** with each other. These sounds include grunts, barks, and screams.

A Day in the Life of a Baboon

In the Evening

Before it gets dark, the baboons make their way back to their sleeping area. There, the adults groom each other again before they climb to the safety of their trees or cliffs, where they are protected from predators. The one predator that baboons fear the most is the leopard—especially at night, when leopards hunt for their **prey**.

Like all other primates, baboons are social animals. This means they live, eat, sleep, and travel in groups that have a common bond. They take care of each other and protect each other—like a family.

Glossary

adapt: To adjust, or change, in order to live in a certain habitat

communicate: To share information; to send a signal

diet: The food that an animal or person usually eats

diverse: Many different kinds of members

groom: To clean

habitats: The places where animals live and grow

independent: Without help

mate: To join with another animal in order to produce offspring

muzzle: An animal's mouth and nose

omnivores: Animals that eat plants and animals

predators: Animals that hunt and kill other animals

prey: Animals that are hunted and eaten by other animals

ruff: A ring of long hair that grows around an animal's neck

Swahili: A language that is spoken in many parts of East Africa

wild: Natural surroundings; not a zoo

Index